Spot the Difference

Animals

Rebecca Rissman

www.raintreepublishers.co.uk
Visit our website to find out more information about Raintree books.

To order:
Phone 0845 6044371
Fax +44 (0) 1865 312263
Email myorders@raintreepublishers.co.uk

Customers from outside the UK please telephone +44 1865 312262

Raintree is an imprint of Capstone Global Library Limited, a company incorporated in England and Wales having its registered office at 7 Pilgrim Street, London, EC4V 6LB – Registered company number: 6695582

First published in hardback in 2009
Paperback edition first published in 2010

Edited by Rebecca Rissman, Sian Smith, and Charlotte Guillain
Designed by Kimberly Miracle and Joanne Malivoire
Picture research by Elizabeth Alexander

Printed and bound in China by Leo Paper Products Ltd.

ISBN 978 0 431 19416 5 (hardback)
13 12 11 10 09
10 9 8 7 6 5 4 3 2 1

ISBN 978 1 406 26498 2 (paperback)
14 13 12
10 9 8 7 6 5 4 3

British Library Cataloguing in Publication Data
Rissman, Rebecca
Animals. - (Can you spot the difference?) (Acorn plus)
1. Animals - Variation - Pictorial works - Juvenile literature
I. Title
A full catalogue record for this book is available from the British Library.

Acknowledgments

The author and publishers are grateful to the following for permission to reproduce copyright material: Alamy pp. **10** (© imagebroker), **11 right** (© Michael Patrick O'Neill), **13 bottom left** (© Maximilian Weinzierl), **18** (© Image Source Pink), **21 left** (© Bruce Coleman INC.); Corbis pp. **17 left** (© Martin Harvey), **17 right** (© Jeffrey L. Rotman); Getty Images pp. **6** (Yasuhide Fumoto/ Stone), **7 bottom left** (George Grall/ National Geographic), **7 right** (Tim Flach/Stone), **11 left** (Zena Holloway/ Taxi), **12** (Gail Shumway/Photographer's Choice), **13 right** (Kevin Horan/Stone), **22 top left** (Yasuhide Fumoto/ Stone), **22 top right** (Tim Flach/Stone); Image Quest 3-D p. **7 top left** (© 2003 Scott Tuason); Photolibrary pp. **8** (Anup Shah/Photodisc), **9 middle** (Stan Osolinski/OSF), **11 middle** (Michael Dick/Animals Animals), **13 top left** (Gerard Soury/ OSF), **15 left** (Diane Miller/ Monsoon Images), **15 middle** (Satoshi Kuribayashi/ OSF), **16** (Jack Goldfarb/Design Pics Inc), **17 middle** (Dale Robert Franz/Imagestate), **19 right** (David Tipling/OSF), **19 top left** (Photolibrary/Per Klaesson/ Scanpix), **20** (Peter Weimann/Animals Animals), **22 bottom right** (Satoshi Kuribayashi/ OSF); Shutterstock pp. **4**, **5** (© abxyz), **9 left** (© clearviewstock), **9 right** (© TheSupe87), **14** (© Mayskyphoto), **15 right** (© kolo5), **19 bottom left** (© Ljupco Smokovski), **21 middle** (© Henk Bentlage), **21 right** (© Loris Eichenberger), **22 bottom left** (© Mayskyphoto).

Cover photographs: Pangolin from © How Hwee Young/epa/ Corbis, flying fox from © javarman/Shutterstock, crocodiles from © Gautier Willaume/Shutterstock, elephant from © salamanderman/Shutterstock, flamingo from © Christian Musat/Shutterstock, green tree python from © Judy Worley/ Shutterstock, Montana brown cottonwood rabbit from © Alan Scheer/Shutterstock, zebra from © Tim Davis/Corbis. Back cover photograph reproduced with permission of Photolibrary (Anup Shah/Photodisc).

We would like to thank Nancy Harris and Adriana Scalise for their help in the preparation of this book.

Every effort has been made to contact copyright holders of any material reproduced in this book. Any omissions will be rectified in subsequent printings if notice is given to the publisher.

Contents

Some words are shown in bold, **like this**. They are explained in "Words to know" on page 23.

Animals

Animals are living things. Animals need food and water to live.

Animals have different body parts to help them live. Animal body parts can be many shapes. Animal body parts can be many sizes.

Eyes

Animals use their eyes to see. Most animals have two eyes on their faces. But animal eyes can look very different!

This squid's eyes are very big. This spider has eight eyes. This tree frog's eyes are bright red.

Ears

Animals use their ears to hear. Most animals have two ears on their heads. But animal ears can look very different!

This lizard's ear looks like a hole. This hare has large ears. This dog's ears are floppy.

Noses

Animals use their noses to smell and **breathe air**. Most animal noses are on their faces. But animal noses can look very different!

This turtle's nose is very small. This monkey's nose is big. This manatee's nose is covered with whiskers.

Mouths

Animals use their mouths to eat and **breathe**. Some animals also use their mouths for **defence**. Most animal mouths are on their faces. But animal mouths can look very different!

This whale shark's mouth is wide. This mouse deer's mouth is small. This snake's mouth is full of sharp teeth called **fangs**.

Wings

Some animals have wings. Most animals use their wings to fly. Some animals have wings but do not fly. Animal wings can look very different!

This egret's wings are long and white. This beetle's wings are **transparent**. This ostrich's wings are big, but it does not fly!

Tails

Many animals have tails. They use their tails to move. They use their tails to balance. But animal tails can look very different!

This iguana's tail is striped. This bobcat's tail is short. This stingray's tail is long and thin. And it has a **barb** at the end!

Legs

Animals use their legs to stand. Animals use their legs to get around. But animal legs can look very different!

This dog's legs are short. This lizard's legs are **scaly**. This sandpiper's legs are thin.

Feet

Animals use their feet to move. Animals use their feet for **defense**. Most animals have feet attached to their legs. But animal feet can look very different!

This mouse's feet are very tiny. This elephant's feet are big. This gecko's feet are sticky.

Spot the Difference!

How many differences can you see?

Words to Know

air gas that humans and many other animals need to breathe in to stay alive. We cannot see the air but it is all around us on Earth.

barb sharp point that can be used like a hook

breathe take in air

compare look at two or more things to see how they are the same and how they are different

defense protecting yourself when attacked

fang long, sharp, pointed tooth

protect keep safe

scaly covered in scales. Scales are thin, overlapping plates that cover the skin of some animals. Most fish are covered in scales.

similar a lot like or nearly the same as another thing

transparent clear or see-through

Index

Note to Parents and Teachers

Before reading

Ask children what types of body parts different animals have. As children are giving examples, create a list on a piece paper. Focus on the following body parts: ears, eyes, feet, nose, mouths, wings, tails, and legs. Go through the chart with the children and ask them if we have any of the listed body parts and what we use them for. Then ask children which body parts only animals have. Ask children what they think animals use those body parts for.

After reading

- Assign children an animal – elephant, pig, horse, bird, snake, and monkey. Children have to find their classmates who are the same animal as them by making the noise that animal would make and without talking. Once they are in their groups, discuss the body parts that make their groups similar or different.

- Have children make individual books or a class book titled "Animal Body Parts". Children can draw various pictures of animals and label the body parts on their drawings. If making individual books, give children pieces of paper with the name of a body part at the top of each page. Children can draw a picture of an animal with that body part.